Archaeology: What You Need to Know

Dr. David Tee

Published by Dr. David Tee, 2020.

Introduction

You may have heard a little about archaeology and may have even seen the many articles in the news detailing the discoveries.

Yet you may not know that much about this scientific research field. Studying history is not the most exciting activity for a majority of people in this world.

They have more pressing concerns which keeps their minds in the present. They do not want to be concerned about the problems that people had 3,000 years ago or even 2,000 years ago.

Although many people are bored with history archaeology can help modern people face their troubles, find the answers they seek as well as help guide their children to be constructive contributing citizens.

The information that the past holds help farmers with their crops get a better yield. That information also helps one adjust their lifestyle to eat better foods for a healthier lifestyle.

Archaeology also helps people live better Christian lives. The people who take the time to read about the past, find that different discoveries build their faith which they then can pass on to their children.

Knowing the answers to little children's questions go a long way in keeping those same children from walking away from their faith and their families.

What follows is a brief discussion on what takes place in the field of archaeology. There is a lot more to the field than making wonderful discoveries.

In fact, there are a lot of personal agendas at work that would undermine the objectives already stated in this section.

Not every archaeologist is a Christian. That means that the average pastor, church leader, missionary and parents should take the time to familiarize themselves with the field of archaeology.

Too many archaeologists have lost their faith when they looked to archaeology over God to sustain their faith.

Archaeology is not infallible, and it is filled with limitations that hinder it from uncovering all the details of the past.

Then different archaeologists with their own theories often distort the physical evidence they uncover and try to have it say what they want it to say.

It is up to the believer to take the initiative and learn about the field of archaeology so they can address controversies, unbelievers' arguments and their own children's questions

This book gives you an overview of what goes on in the realm of archaeological work. It is written to help the reader become more aware of what goes on in the field and helps them be more wary when someone says the events of the Bible did not take place.

It is also written so that the unwary believer can be more alert and protect their own faith when unbelieving archaeologists declare the Bible wrong.

God wants his people to gain knowledge, but that knowledge has to be the truth. God's people are not to be repeating misinformation nor take any information blindly.

They need to be equipped to handle archaeological discoveries as God would want. The way to do that is to follow God's word over science.

You can't do that if you do not know much about the field of archaeology as it is one tool that is used to mislead God's people and call their faith a lie.

Just so you know, archaeology actually supports the Bible, contrary to what many archaeologists and other unbelievers claim.

Keep that in mind as you read these pages.

Archaeology and Faith

Archaeology Digs up old cultures

Archaeology and archaeologists have done wonders uncovering our human history throughout the years. A recent discovery at Gath has shown that there was much more to the city than originally thought.

It lay hidden for the 23 years the chief archaeologist, Aren Maier, has dug at the site. With nothing against Dr. Maier, the question rises 'was this actually an original city constructed by the Philistines or was it in existence when the Philistine immigrated to the Levant?'[1]

This is one of the things we learn through archaeology. Nothing is as it seems. Unfortunately, while we now have this new discovery, this is not a complete picture pf what transpired in the era of Gath and the Philistines.

There is still too much information missing that hinders archaeologists from drawing a complete picture.

The information is not there

There is in archaeology an element that keeps us from knowing exactly what the discovery is about and from learning a complete picture about the past.

Kenneth Kitchen wrote in the first chapter of his book, The Bible in Its World, of this destructive element. In his examples, erosion was the main culprit and this natural destructive force was seen in destroying over 95% of a given site.[2]

This, of course, is not the only natural destructive force that archaeology and archaeologists have to contend with.

There are wars, earthquakes, sandstorms, rain storms and a lot more that all play a role in destroying sites that existed thousands of years ago.

To draw conclusions about our history based upon roughly 2 to 5 % of the actual remains is not a rational method to use.

Yet, that is what is done and has been done for over the roughly 2 centuries the field of archaeology has been in existence. Archaeologists tend to draw conclusions based on incomplete data and some of those conclusions have influenced many a believing archaeologist away from their biblical faith. They use the absence of evidence to influence their life's decisions and take them away from a belief that God and the Bible are to an idea that neither are true.[3]

Some very prominent scholars and archaeologists have used the lack of information archaeology has uncovered to turn their faith in God around and lead them away from salvation. James Strange and William Dever are two examples of this common decision.[4]

The latter was an ordained minister and pastored a church for over a decade while the former does not believe in the physical reality of the resurrection of Jesus. These changes in their beliefs are because of what they did not find when they were full time archaeologists.[5]

Part of the reason why these men and women lose their faith is because they put too much faith in the research field and expect it to perform miracles.

No research field can and with the limitations of archaeology it is unrealistic to expect it to deliver mind boggling discoveries that ensure people will fall down and worship God or change from an atheist, agnostic or a simple unbeliever into a believer.

Archaeology cannot produce what has been removed from existence. So, to base one's belief on what cannot be found instead of looking at what has been uncovered is not the most intelligent way to use the field.

This is the danger that many young people are faced with. They are taught by those professors who do not believe God's word or have had it destroyed because what they were expecting did not turn up.

This biased influence them influences those young minds, Christians included, and gets them on the path to disbelieving God and his word.

What needs to be done is for people to focus on those discoveries that have shown that God and the Bible have told the truth. The museums are full of such discoveries.

Their value cannot be diminished simply because an archaeologist working 2,000 to 5,000 years after the fact did not find what they wanted to find.

As Kenneth Kitchen has said and it is a statement that has been repeated by many other scholars and archaeologists, 'the absence of evidence is not evidence for absence'[6]

One's faith should not be based on what cannot be found but on the word of God. Archaeology is merely a tool to help people strengthen their faith in God by what it does find.

Their faith should be based on the word of God and the fact that he cannot lie.[7] A limited research field like archaeology cannot produce the physical evidence needed to show that God did not tell the truth.

The Problem of Objectivity

In archaeology, there is supposed to be some type of practice that keeps personal beliefs, preferences and bias out of analyzing the different discoveries. After all it is supposed to be a science and science practices objectivity. At least in name they do.[8]

Yet, this scientific principle is often ignored, and that act tends to influence the conclusions and theories about different discoveries. Different schools of thought, the Maximalist and the Minimalist, disagree on which parts of the Bible are true and their individual ideologies influence their actions and how different discoveries apply to the biblical record.[9]

There is little objectivity participating in the field of archaeology. An archaeologists' view will depend on how he or she views the contents of the Bible or if they have any real belief in God or not.

The Bible tells us that we cannot serve two masters. We must choose which one we will follow and obey. That verse is telling us that there is no such thing as real objectivity. One's views will be influenced by their personal views.[10]

Some archaeologists have grown wise to that fact and that is why we have two different schools of thought when it comes to the biblical record.

In his book, Did God have a Wife, Dr. Wm. Dever made a big point out of how no one really believes that objectivity is possible or even exists. He feels so strongly about it that he mentioned that objectivity is not the goal of his book or archaeology. In his book, he was giving his readers his point of view as he saw them.[11]

So, this means that the conclusions about every discovery are going to have to views or conclusions attached to them. There will be the view of the archaeologist who made the discovery and created his hypothesis about it. Then there will be the view of those who disagrees with that thought or hypothesis.

The non-archaeologist is then left up to decide which view they will believe and accept and which one they will reject and not believe.

But what weakens Dr. Dever's stand about objectivity is the double standard that permeates the field of archaeology. There are those who will apply the 'there is no such thing as objectivity' argument when talking about those manuscripts, artifacts and other discoveries that they person is going along with. But when the topic turns to the biblical authors, they are dismissed as not being objective. Dr. Dever calls their writings propaganda not honest writing.[12]

This is what makes doing biblical archaeology very difficult. As one the one hand you have a group of people saying that objectivity is impossible and agreeing with God on the issue.

Then when the biblical record is raised, these same people demand that the biblical writers, modern Christians and believing archaeologists be objective in their conclusions, theories and so on.

While she is not known for her Christianity, Eilat Mazar discovered what she identified as King David's temple. There was nothing wrong with her identification and it was made follow archaeological rules and principles. Yet, that did not stop Israel Finkelstein from visiting the site and contradicting her identification. He and several other minimalist archaeologists wrote a paper on the topic.[13]

This competing thinking by experts of equal status can be confusing to those who are outside the field of archaeology and have little knowledge of what really goes on inside that research area.

Jesus told us that we would know the truth so we must depend on that instruction to help get to the bottom of the confusing issues that constantly arise in archaeology.

To help get to the truth, we must consider the source. A couple questions need to be asked- 1). What are the spiritual beliefs of the archaeologists involved? And 2). what archaeological point of view do they side with?

Since there is no objectivity in this world, these questions are not going to be hard to answer.

To get to the bottom of the debate, one must lean on God to help direct one to the truth. Sometimes unbelieving archaeologists will acknowledge much of the Bible making it even harder to find out which theory is correct.

Sometimes both sides can be wrong, and we must keep digging to find the right answer to the problem.

The key in this debate is to be honest. An archaeologist or student of history has to make sure they have what they think they have before announcing it to the world.

Being honest offsets the lack of objectivity issue.

Archaeology's Limitations

The lack of objectivity is not the sole archaeological limitation that makes it difficult to glean information from the past.

There are a lot of physical realities that interfere with the investigation of the past. These realities cannot be overcome with any modification to the field of research no matter how advanced the technology.

One of the main limitations is that archaeology is known as a destructive research field. It is one of the few scientific fields where the work conducted cannot be redone and tested through a variety of means and methods. Once a site is excavated that is it. Even if an archaeologist wants to correct a mistake, he cannot do that. What was there is now gone.[14]

Another limitation is a religious one. While it is physical it is a human limitation imposed on archaeologists from the ultra-orthodox Jewish religious group. These people do not like to see the bones disturbed during any archaeological dig and take to extreme measures to keep the bones from being examined. Whether it be political pressure or death threats, this group places a big limitation on what can or cannot be done in archaeology in Israel. The groups motivations are questioned, and it has been said that their actions are based on less than honorable intentions.[15]

On top of these limitations there are more realistic and natural ones that make discovering the past and what went on very difficult. It is not the subjective nature of the archaeologist's interpretation of what took place. There are four major limitations that slows the discovery of the past as outlined by Dr. Edwin Yamauchi. The first is that what is uncovered is a minute portion of a minute percentage of what was made. The second is very few of the ancient sites have been found, and of those that have, have not been surveyed. The third limitation is that of all the sites identified, maybe less than 3% have actually been excavated. Those that have have barely touched the surface of the remains. Finally, very little of the material uncovered has been analyzed and published so data and information is lacking.[16]

What really makes archaeology limited is the fact that the field and its practitioners cannot reconstruct what is gone. By that it is meant that the destructive elements found in this world have taken their toll on archaeological remains and permanently removed the items from existence. Invading armies and their rulers have often destroyed artifacts from conquered societies. Some, like the ancient Egyptians, have altered their texts to present a better view of their era for future generations. And on it goes.[17]

Kenneth Kitchen has detailed some of these destructive elements in his book, On the Reliability of the Old Testament, when he wrote that the East Delta was so moist that almost all of the written records for the 13th century BC are completely gone. It doesn't matter what the contents were, papyrus does not survive in that part of Egypt and archaeology cannot resurrect the lost evidence.[18]

As noted earlier, another of Mr. Kitchen's books takes the whole first chapter to outline other destructive forces that also permanently remove archaeological buildings as well. It is not just papyrus and other writing materials that are vulnerable to all of these destructive elements that limit the research capability of archaeology.[19]

This is not to exclude the natural disasters like sandstorms, earthquakes, floods and more that bury the ancient remains or totally destroys them.

These acts of nature are out of the control of the archaeologist and they do not know what has been removed from the possibility of discovery.

They have been at work for thousands of years, leaving no trace of the people, their material culture, or their cities or nations.

Even though archaeology is known to be a destructive force at least its destruction leaves artifacts, manuscripts and buildings that can be seen and examined many times over.

It also leaves hordes of pottery finds, some of which have been used to inscribe different daily activities on them when paper wasn't available.

Archaeology has its limits that is why the archaeologist and the public need to be careful when they use this field to declare that God and the Bible are wrong.

We are only getting a very tiny look at the past and one that is far from the complete picture. Also, miracles like Joshua's stationary sun, the miracles of Jesus, and later Peter and the disciples leave no archaeological evidence behind to show that they took place.

These supernatural acts cannot fit into archaeology's scope as the term means study of ancient remains. Not the study of all things that took place in history.

As noted earlier, many archaeologists and bible scholars, as well as pastors, missionaries, and laymen have made negative eternal decisions based upon what archaeology has not uncovered.

They place their faith in a very limited scientific field that cannot hope to produce all the information they want to see.

This is a bad mistake as God did not say use physical evidence to base one's faith upon. He said the just shall live by faith. He also said that the use of proper faith pleases him.

While faith in God and the Bible will get some physical evidence to keep it going and strong, it will not get so much that it destroys the purpose of faith and ruin what pleases God.

The limitations of archaeology should remind everyone of this fact. Then what archaeology does uncover can be used properly to build faith instead of tearing it down and leading people away from both God and the truth.

The Issue of Archaeological Forgeries

It goes without saying that forgeries occur in archaeology as it does in just about any endeavor in life. People like to forge different items for whatever reason they have, and archaeology is not excluded from that club.

One thing that needs to be noted is that forgery is not a modern monopoly. It has taken place in the past including ancient times. In fact, the Romans made a law against forging their money back in about 81 BC. The punishment if slaves were caught forging coins was death. But free men or Roman citizens would only be banished.[20]

This fact that archaeology is not immune to any act of forgery concerns the archaeological and academic world greatly. It has caused at least one publication, Biblical Archaeology Review, to stop publishing articles that focus on those discoveries that have no legitimate paper trail or what is called provenance.[21]

This decision was made by the new editor of BAR inspite of the feelings and actions of the previous editor and founder of BAR, Hershel Shanks. He wanted to get to the truth behind the unprovenanced artifacts and would not hesitate to publish articles that explored the questionable artifacts.[22]

The issue of forgery though has not been far from Mr. Shanks' mind as in 2007 he organized and conducted a council on forgery and unprovenanced discoveries in Jerusalem. This conference was attended by many top names in ancient scholarship and archaeology.[23]

What came of this report and conference was basically the feelings, opinions of these experts but very little can be done to stop the flow of forged materials.

The problem comes in when any expert lends their education and expertise in authenticating what turns out to be a forgery.

Embarrassment is the least of the expert's problems. Although it may not be avoided as forgery identification can be very subjective with experts relying on information outside of their field of expertise to draw their conclusions.[24]

This subjectivity can be seen in how a committee is selected to determine if an artifact is forged or not. This is not a committee who knows little about archaeology and only listens to expert testimonies to get to the truth. These types of committees are comprised of experts who know archaeology very well and know about the items under scrutiny. This situation then can produce varying and often contrary opinions about the questionable artifact.[25]

Determining whether a discovered manuscript, diary or piece of pottery is a forgery is based on the experts' opinion.

This leads us back to the concept of provenance.

The idea of not publishing any ancient artifact, etc., because the provenance is not known is seen as one weapon in stopping forged materials from entering the archaeological realm.

To be able to publish or have seen any discovery as archaeologically sound and legitimate, the discoverer must produce verifiable evidence of the origin of the item. Failing to provide this evidence makes the item under review suspect of being a forgery.[26]

Many accusations are hurled at the owner of the artifact including using archaeologists as means to up the value and sell the item at a profit. Or that the item was looted from an archaeological site and sent to the black market first. Finally, the item can be accused as being a forgery rendering its valueless.[27]

The strong stand against unprovenanced discoveries poses a problem for the archaeologist and the archaeological world.

If ignored and left unpublished vital information about the past could be excluded and a complete picture of our history is doomed to be incomplete.

Sometimes, as in the case of the James Ossuary, the information on the artifact is rejected because it confirms a biblical truth or event. The James Ossuary held the highly contentious inscription that James was the brother of Jesus. There was a year's long trial over this inscription trying to confirm its legitimacy or forged nature.[28]

To outright dismiss any discovery because it did not come through approved archaeological channels is playing fast and loose with archaeological remains.

Some investigation into these discovered items is needed if it is hoped to recover important information about the different ancient societies.

There are several professional organizations that are refusing to deal with unprovenanced finds.

The Society of Biblical Literature is just one of those organizations, but their attitude is not good for archaeology as a whole. The reason for this stance is to stop the looting that takes place.[29]

There are just too many archaeological sites left unattended because there are not enough archaeologists available to excavate them.

Because of the economic factor in the region, looting is not going to stop any time soon. Not with the amount of dollars available that private collectors pay out for genuine artifacts.

Another method must be adopted so information about the past is not lost permanently.

Amateurs Outdo the Experts

It would be something if all archaeological discoveries, especially the important ones, were all made by the experts and professional archaeologists.

This way we would avoid the arguments of authenticity, forgery and other accusations that undermine the credibility of the discovery or push it off into the background of archaeological work.

Yet the ideal way of making discovery often eludes professional archaeologists. The major discoveries have mostly been made accidentally and by people not even closely associated with the research field.

It has gotten so bad that back in 2007 Eric Cline, a seasoned archaeologist and scholar wrote an editorial that complains about the many amateurs invading the field of archaeology and making claims of great archaeological discoveries.[30]

He laments in that article about the lack of scientific and archaeological training these amateurs have and had. He lists a few of the amateurs and their lack of credentials but his article sounds more like a person who is jealous of the success that seems to elude many professional archaeologists.[31]

Unfortunately for Mr. Cline and the many professional archaeologists and Bible scholars who spend their free time digging in the dirt, amateurs have uncovered many artifacts that have turned out to be vital to archaeology in general.

One of the first major discoveries that came by the hand of the amateur was the Rosetta Stone.

This stone was found by an engineer who traveled with Napoleon to Egypt in 1798. The stone was uncovered accidentally when the engineer was digging in the area of Rosetta. The stone measures only 3 feet 9 inches by 2 feet 4 inches in size and is about 11 inches thick. But the 3 inscriptions on it, lead to the deciphering of Egyptian hieroglyphics which were on the known ancient Egyptian monuments at the time. Because ancient Greek was inscribed on the stone, it was only a matter of time before scholars could read what the ancient Egyptians had written.[32]

Then just under a century later, the Amarna letters were uncovered in 1887. Unfortunately for the professional archaeologists at the time, it was a Bedouin woman who was walking along the riverbank who made the accidental yet very important discovery. Because the Bedouin tribesmen dug up the approx. 300 tablets, the archaeological world rejected the discovery. What these letters contained was royal Egyptian correspondence from Akhenaten's father Amenophis III to other rulers.[33]

Due to the attitude towards looting at that time, valuable information was lost. The information contained in those letters shed light on ancient international relations and could have helped archaeologists to learn more about how different societies worked and interacted with each other.[34]

The 20th century was not going to be outdone by previous ones. This century saw the amateur discovery of 2 of the greatest archaeological finds of all times.

The first was the Nag Hammadi Library in 1945. This set of ancient codexes laid buried for about 2000 years, at least to our knowledge, until it was discovered by Egyptians collecting fertilizer near the community of Nag Hammadi. Inside the jars found by these Egyptians were about 13 books now called the Nag Hammadi Library. Unfortunately, those codexes were subject to further damage as the Egyptians did not know what they had found. There is a long story to the library's journey from discovery to prominence but through it all many Gnostic works can be studied freely.[35]

The second great discovery was in Israel near Qumran. The Dead Sea Scrolls were uncovered in 1947. It seems that every article and every book written about these scrolls contain the discovery story. This will not be repeated here. Suffice it to say that a goat tender accidentally made the discovery through a method that professional archaeologists never use. The Dead Sea Scrolls were probably the most important discovery of any time because it showed the world that the text of the Bible had not changed from ancient times till now.[36]

These are only a few of the important discoveries made by amateurs. If Mr. Cline had his way, these and other important discoveries would never be made.

Or if they were, they may suffer a worst fate than the Amarna Letters given the modern attitude if refusing to even look at those unprovenanced artifacts.

But even with so many great archaeological discoveries made by amateurs, it does not mean that the professionals do not come across very important finds.

One such discovery is the Tel Dan Stele uncovered through a professional excavation conducted by Avraham Biran. This discovery was made in 2 parts. The first fragment was discovered in 1993. Almost a year later 2 more fragments were found, and these discoveries fit the original almost perfectly. Once joined together scholars versed in Aramaic could read the account. It is one of the earliest non-biblical mentioning of the people of Israel and Judah. It also mentions the words 'House of David' which provides extra biblical support for the biblical record.[37]

It is granted that amateurs should take more care in recording their finds, but if they do, they may expose a whole network of looters. Forgers and the people who purchase those finds.

But we cannot dismiss amateur discoveries nor bar amateurs from making discoveries. Too much information is lost when people like Mr. Cline try to ban others from doing the exact same thing he does on a yearly basis.

They may not practice good scientific and archaeological methods, but those methods are often lacking as they leave far too much information buried for future archaeologists.

This forfeiture only enables the distorted conclusions archaeologists make of the past. The practice of leaving items buried in the dirt is not helping anyone.

Archaeological reports

There are two types of archaeological reports. One is the yearly report that is done to summarize the season's activities and state the archaeologist's vision.

Dr. Steven Collins used to place his annual reports on his dig's website, Tall el-Hamman excavation project. Those reports seemed to have been moved now but if you read one, you would see two main cha5racteristics about them. They are very boring filled with a lot of technical information and vocabulary and they stated that Dr. Collins believes his site is the location of Biblical Sodom.[38]

The other kind of report is what is called the final report. This written work is usually done when the excavation has been completed and that may take several years to do.

When the excavation is over, the lead archaeologist is supposed to write a final report. That is the ideal at any rate. This has become what is known as one of archaeology's problems. Those reports are rarely done in a timely manner.

For example, Dr. Dever finally got to writing his final report on his work at Gezer, in 2015. 40 years after he had finished his excavations at the site. Whatever information Dr. Dever had on the site was kept hidden from other professional archaeologists and the public for 4 decades.[39]

He is not alone in this as there was a married couple who also waited 40 years to write and publish their final report. In fact, this has become what has been called 'archaeology's dirty little secret'. Archaeologists for whatever reason they may have refuse to write their final reports and leave the world guessing as to what they found, their interpretations and other important data.[40]

Some final reports have been written long after the lead archaeologist has died. One prime example is the celebrated Israeli archaeologist Benjamin Mazar. His work at the Ophel was delayed long after his death and was not written until his granddaughter took it up and published it for him[41]

Another important archaeologist, Kathleen Kenyon never wrote her final report on her work at Jericho. In fact, it was written 30 years after she finished working at the site and a long 12 years after she died. Her work and data could not be analyzed till the report was made available for everyone. It wasn't till about 2008 that Dr. Bryant Wood went through it and found some errors in her work and conclusions.[42]

There is a very good reason for some of the delays. Many archaeologists prefer to dig instead of writing reports. That is a very understandable reason as when the archaeologists doesn't dig, the information remains buried until who knows when it will be uncovered. In the case of Dr. Avarham Biren's case, his report was delayed because he kept making great discoveries at Tel Dan. Unfortunately, he died not too long ago, and it was left to his staff to write and publish a final report on their work.[43]

But it is not just archaeologists that refuse or fail to publish their findings. The Dead Sea Scrolls went through a very tumultuous period where the scrolls and fragments were divided up among a select group of scholars. These scholars held a monopoly over the scrolls and refused to publish their findings, their opinions and so on. One scholar worked on one small fragment for 11 years and was still; not near publishing his work or the fragment. It took a lot of work by Hershel Shanks to get that monopoly broken and for the scrolls to be seen by other than the assigned scholars. The story of this battle is recorded in Mr. Shanks book freeing the Dead Sea Scrolls.[44]

The withholding of this information does not do anyone one any good. It may feed the egos of the archaeologists and the scholars but that is no reason to hide any data when there are people waiting to hear what has been discovered and what is their significance to their lives and beliefs.

Another issue in this is where these scholars publish. If they restrict their publications to scholarly magazines and journals, then only a few people will see their work and conclusions.

The rest of the world will be left in the dark and they may even hold some resentment. They will also hold to less valuable, realistic and factual commentary on the different subjects those reports speak on.[45]

This lack of publishing outside of archaeology's accepted publications can lead to depriving the public of the truth. This is something that the public desperately needs. Wild tails of aliens and other unrealistic theories can be defended against if the real data could actually be read and digested.

Publication would certainly help pastors and Christian teachers as they get the information they need to help their congregations and students thrive and grow as Christians.

Scholars and archaeologists can always publish preliminary final reports with the caveat that the information may change as more work is done on the archaeological sites.

If the archaeologist is honest, there is no harm getting the information out there for all to see.

There is No Smoking Gun

You may hear from unbelievers that archaeology has upended the biblical accounts and proved them untrue.

This is not so. While some scientists say they have smoking gun evidence that renders the words of God moot, they are merely pretending and doing wishful thinking. Even the secondary crater they declare to be the smoking gun that proves the dinosaurs were wiped out by an asteroid hitting the earth some 65 million years ago.[46]

Unfortunately for those scientists they are mistaken in their assumption and conclusion. The supposed crater that they claim was partly responsible for that scientific tragedy actually cannot be seen. It is buried beneath a kilometer of other rocks and debris.[47]

There is another problem for these scientists other than their smoking gun evidence being buried and incapable of being seen.

What is also wrong is that this supposed crater cannot be verified creating the results the scientists said took place.

There are no ancient documents to corroborate the scientists claims, no documents from any era saying that asteroids hit the earth and more.

This situation remains a common theme throughout the evolutionary side of earth's history. It is repeated over and over with the same story undermining all the claims evolutionary scientists make.

None of those types of claims can be verified. Also, scientists, archaeologists and biblical scholars do not have stored away in any museum around the world one single artifact, piece of pottery or other discovery that proves the Bible untrue.

The archaeological world is not that large. If someone had uncovered such a piece of evidence, the whole archaeological world would hear about it and rush to the site where the artifact. etc., was stored wanting to examine it.

There is no such artifact or archaeological discovery that could be described as a smoking gun piece of evidence.

Dr. Nelson Gleuck stated that there had been no archaeological discovery that upended any part of the Bible and shown it to be false. [48] Since his time, and he died in 1971, there still has not been one archaeological discovery that has proven the Bible false.

With thousands of archaeological digs taking place almost every year and more than a thousand archaeologists searching that is quite a feat.

But what Dr. Gleuck said was not the complete quote. He went on to state that up to his time, there have been scores of discoveries proving the Bible true in its historical records. He also stated that when the Bible is understood correctly, the descriptions found in the Bible led to more discoveries. In other words, the idea of a smoking gun is an unrealistic hope and impossibility.[49]

If there is anything trying to prove the Biblical record untrue, it is the archaeologist's assumptions, leaps to conclusions, their hypothesis, their conjecture and theories.

All of those are based upon vulnerable evidence, which has the archaeologists' or biblical scholars' personal views read into what is uncovered.

These ideas are not based in fact nor in the evidence itself. Those concepts are what the archaeologist wants the past to be instead of what the past was actually like.

When an archaeologist creates his assumption, etc., about his excavation or even a sole artifact he or she usually ends up using their interpretative skills. They are not taking the truth out of the discovery. Instead they are reading into the discovery what they want it to say and they do this through their use of interpretation.

Their own set of biases, lack of belief or beliefs and so on, alter what the artifact or other discovery is really saying. These elements often mislead the identification and lead the archaeologist or bible scholar down the wrong path to the wrong conclusion.[50]

You can search all the archaeological museums in the world, making sure to go through their storerooms that are filled with pottery, etc., and even spend a decade doing it. But you will never find any smoking gun that shows the bible to be untrue.

Like that unseen crater any piece of smoking gun evidence touted by unbelieving scientists and archaeologists cannot be substantiated.

The Bible contains the ancient documentation that supports the discoveries which support it.

The archaeologists' leaps to conclusion are not given that kind of support.

Is it Biblical Archaeology or Not

The world of archaeology is not filled or even led by true believers. If it were, then the research field might have more clarity and a more honest view of the past.

It is hard to say when biblical archaeology got its name and its own sub field in the general research field called archaeology but the term biblical has been used ever since Edward Robinson published his work in roughly the year 1939.[51]

A good definition of this field of research is that biblical archaeology is designed to discover data, information, artifacts and other physical evidence that would provide a clearer understanding and knowledge of the people, cities, etc., mentioned in the Bible. This definition limits the scope of Biblical Archaeology which has rankled other members who dig in the same countries as those mentioned in the Bible.[52]

The name Syro-Palestine archaeology is not new. Dr. WH Albright made it a sub field of Biblical Archaeology as the latter was far more important in scope. Although he was not the father of this research focus. He gave credit to Frederick Bliss. No matter who founded the filed, under Dr. Albright's influence Syro-Palestine Archaeology was relegated to a small area and that may have been the right choice as the Biblical period overshadows much of any ancient Syro-Palestine er.[53]

But not all archaeologists are satisfied with Dr. Albright's classification and have tried to put Biblical Archaeology under the auspices of Syro-Palestine Archaeology instead. Dr. Wm. Dever is a champion of this movement and opposition to Biblical Archaeology became known in 1074 when he established a school for Syro-Palestine archaeology and attacked the very nature of Biblical Archaeology. Dr. Dever's feelings at the time were that the name should have been demoted to something like 'archaeology of the biblical period' or 'archaeology of the Bible'.[54]

But Dr. Dever is not the only one in this battle over Biblical Archaeology. It is said that the field has now become filled with those who do not believe the Bible and seek to prove it untrue at every chance they get. It is the Bible and not only Biblical Archaeology that is under attack with this battle for a name change and demotion of Biblical Archaeology to be a sub field of Syro-Palestine Archaeology.[55]

There has long been an accusation that the bible believing archaeologists, in the early days of Biblical Archaeology, went about their exploration and excavations with a Bible in one hand a trowel in the other.

It is a baseless charge because the Bible is one of the few ancient texts that actually has locations of long-lost cities that dotted the ancient landscape.

Without the Bible, many of those cities would not be discovered and probably still lay hidden under the sand allowing unbelieving archaeologists and scholars to claim the Bible is in error.

They can't do this because the Bible has led to so many discoveries because of its rich and detailed descriptions of different locations. What is also important to know is that in return for helping different archaeologists find these lost locations, archaeology has proven that the Bible has placed the different nations, cities and figures in the right era and location.[56]

The Bible is not being proven false by archaeological discoveries. But does this mean that Biblical Archaeology should have its own classification and that Syro-Palestine archaeology be classified as a sub field as Dr. Albright had said?

The importance of Biblical Archaeology is clear. Without the help of God and his written word there would be less physical evidence supporting the believer's faith in God and the Bible.

It doesn't matter if the archaeologist is holding the Bible in one hand while he or she does their exploration. The Bible has been proven to be a great aid in finding ancient Kingdoms, and so on.

The Bible cannot be tossed out like an old rag just because some unbelievers do not want or are willing to accept the help.

Science on its own does not have the information needed to help archaeologists locate a given site.

Extra biblical records that talk about those sites, were often not uncovered till people followed the Bible to the right spots and started to excavate.

The field should remain named Biblical Archaeology as the name gives the work purpose, direction and a proven source for the locations of long-lost villages and empires.

If people want to have it named Syro-Palestine Archaeology, then the focus would change as would the purpose. Biblical finds would be relegated to lesser priorities as many archaeologists seek information on the people who also occupied the Levant and surrounding areas.

The fight over the name is probably a fight over what Biblical Archaeology reminds unbelievers. That there is a God who created all things and cares not only about his chosen people but all of his creation. In other words, removing the term Biblical Archaeology helps unbelievers hide from the truth. They do not want to be reminded of the eternal implications that comes with the Bible through all the discoveries made by those who participate in the field of Biblical Archaeology.[57]

Pseudo Archaeology

There are many different types of people involved with archaeology. Some are legitimately trained professionals who have taken years to learn ancient language and so on.

Then there are those who are on the fringe. Some, sad to say, are very religious people who may be earnest in their work yet completely misguided in how they pursue the field.

These are not the serious Christian archaeologists who support the biblical record but those like Ron Wyatt and Simcha Jacobovici who make claims that cannot be proven.

A third group would be the those who think aliens once visited the earth only to help mankind develop structures that science cannot explain today. Erich van Danikan is probably the most well-known person involved in this group.

The people involved in these groups form what is called Pseudoarchaeology. This branch of archaeology is simple false archaeology. It is pursuing an agenda using archaeology as justification for their wild theories about items that cannot be explained today.[58]

Yes, it is true that there is a lot of well-meaning people out there who misuse the research field. Their work only makes it tougher for real archaeologists to get their work done. Their voice is often overshadowed by the voices of these who make claims they cannot support with any real evidence. They read into different artifacts the idea of aliens, etc., because the discoveries surpass the idea modern people have about ancient cultures.[59]

There are some mainstream archaeologists and those who work in archaeology related fields that think that the pseudo archaeologist is a danger. That is because these people do not just create their abnormal hypothesis out of thin air. They use science to add an element of credibility to their thinking. They also create an image that they are fighting mainstream science in order to get the truth out.[60]

It is true that a lot of mainstream archaeologists and scientists do oppose the work and conclusions made by these fringe groups. These people also oppose any archaeological work that supports the Bible, calling it bad archaeology. Their minds are firmly in the secular scientific aspect of archaeology which makes it hard to convince them to see any alternative than their accepted point of view.[61]

The problem with the pseudo archaeologist is that they do not have the physical or documentary evidence to support their views. They take an oddly looking piece of sculpture and read into the remains ideas that have been found only in science fiction. Forgetting that questions like 'why did the aliens only visit that time period and have not continued to visit this planet?'[62]

While people are free to believe whatever they feel like, God has certainly given them the ability of free choice, the real danger comes in when members of the unwary public fall for these scams.

Then they jump on board the alien or that Noah's Ark has been discovered bandwagon and refuse to listen to common sense or even the truth.

The other problem is when legitimate Biblical Archaeology is lumped in with those fringe Christian researchers, and the work done by legitimate Christian archaeologists is painted with the same brush. The truth gets hidden because some mainstream archaeologist has a bias against the Bible and Christians. They seek to limit the field hiding it in another discipline of archaeology so that the discoveries proving the Bible true are not heard over the roar of disbelief that mainstream unbelieving archaeologists hold to.[63]

Instead of pseudo archaeologists using archaeology to promote their theories and conclusions, mainstream unbelieving archaeologists use pseudo archaeology to rid themselves of a legitimate alternative to their accepted secular hypothesis about the past.

This mentality is what makes it difficult for legitimate Christian archaeologists to have their thoughts and discoveries heard or even accepted by secular practitioners of archaeology.

Christians are not the only ones who have to endure this bias against their work. There are many archaeologists who try to boost the credibility of their home country. Their work is often categorized as pseudo archaeology because it is claimed the data has been faked or it is being used to make their nations' history look better than it was. The only trouble here is that this attitude is selectively applied.[64]

Not every nation runs afoul of this and the Bosnian Pyramid is a shining example of how a pseudo archaeologist tries to boost his nation's standing in the world by making claims he cannot support with real archaeological evidence.[65]

The ancient Egyptians seem to be given a pass as their remains is treated as very believable even though it has been proven that the ancient Egyptians often changed their history to make sure their descendants could be proud of their country and their history.[66]

While there are those who do practice pseudo archaeology and their works and conclusions should be ignored, this label is used more to keep people from learning the truth.

This label becomes a convenient tool to dismiss what legitimate Christian and Jewish archaeologist find that show that the Bible is not a book of fables.

A little sophistication is needed on the part of the believers to see through this trend to make sure that they do not throw out honest, credible and true information.

The believer cannot just take the word of the secular archaeologist as they are not the ones who follow the spirit of truth to where the truth lies.

They are following a different master who blinds their eyes and influences their thinking so that they remain deceived.

Education, experience and knowledge of ancient languages are not enough to discover the truthful information different excavations hold.

That takes true Christian archaeologists who do legitimate archaeology.

Similar Histories

Archaeology has uncovered some wonderful things that help show the validity and truthfulness of the Bible.

It has also uncovered information that makes it difficult for some people to accept the biblical stories found in the Bible.

Two of those discoveries involve argon the Great, an ancient king, and Mithras, an ancient founder of an alternative religion. Their stories mirror two people found in the Bible. For Sargon his birth resembles the birth of Moses. Sargon's own words relate how he was placed in a basket of reeds and floated in the Euphrates. He was found not by the king's daughter but a humble gardener.[67]

The similarity in stories has some scholars believing that the supposed biblical editors copied from the ancient Akkadian story and made Moses better than he was.

The same thinking is applied to the birth of Jesus as the story unearthed by archaeologists and scholars has Mithras being born on Dec. 25th, as well as being born of a virgin. Mithras is also said to have a last supper, a death and resurrection. There were other similarities as well.[68]

These discoveries could have uninformed and unwary believers questioning the validity of the biblical stories attached to both Moses and Jesus.

That is if the believer decides to accept the unbeliever's version of events without realizing that it is the unbeliever that does not have divine instructions to be holy and to tell the truth.

The unbelievers do not have a moral code or a supreme being that forbids lying and dishonesty. They have a lot of latitude in their lives that lets them be free to take from the bible those stories and place them on the lives of their heroes and spiritual leaders.[69]

They are free to take from the Bible whatever information they want and edit the words of their kings and religious leaders.

They do this for a variety of reasons one may be that they want to show their people that their secular leaders have divine origins and power.

For the biblical authors to copy from secular works would be unthinkable and sin. The very act would destroy every word found in the Bible rendering salvation and our hope useless.

Yes, we have similar stories, but it is the secular royal records and false religions that do the copying. The Bible tells us that God does not lie thus to copy secular stories would undermine that fact and make God worse than evil itself.

God calls us to be holy because he is holy. That call would be rendered moot if God allowed sin and lies to be a part of his word. He would not be holy either.

That is a lot to think about, and there is more. Throughout history, scholars have claimed that the biblical authors have copied from other scrolls, fables, myths and so on.[70]

The only trouble with that thinking is that one, they leave out God and his promise to preserve his word.

And two, the ancient Israelites did not have a reputation for copying. No one in the ancient world wrote about how the

Jewish people copied their works or even accused the biblical writers of copying. There is no ancient manuscript detailing the act or how it was carried out. It is only assumed by modern unbelieving scholars and archaeologists that the biblical authors copied from other sources. While the Bible does record references to different works, that referencing does not mean that the biblical authors copied from secular nations.[71]

There were an ancient people who did have a reputation for copying. They were the Old Babylonians and it is said they copied everything they could get their hands on. But even the presence of a nation who did copy does not mean that the people of Israel did the same thing. There is just no evidence supporting the accusation.[72]

The fact that Mithraism was a mystery religion means that we do not know what the original beliefs of the followers were, nor do we know the true story about Mithras. He and his followers could change their beliefs at will and no one would be the wiser except those involved in the false religion.[73]

Neither Christianity nor Judaism are secret religions. Everyone can read the Bible and attend a service in either house of worship for both beliefs and see for themselves what both faiths are all about.

With the wealth of ancient biblical manuscripts everyone can also see the original accounts and that they have not changed over the years.

That reality makes it very hard for anyone to copy a king's autobiography or a false religion.

Keep in mind that when the gospels were written, there were still believing and unbelieving eyewitnesses around that could challenge the authors if they wrote anything that was false.

The charge of copying points to the unbelievers and not to God and his biblical authors.

The Archaeological Eras

It is possible that some people not familiar with archaeology will think that this system is fairly infallible.

They may come to that conclusion as they hear various experienced archaeologists use it all the time to date their discoveries.

The Three Age system is made up of the Stone, Bronze and iron eras that archaeologists claim come in a distinct order. The Stone was first, the Bronze was the next step up in development and the Iron was the last developmental stage in ancient history. This set of eras was originated by a Danish museum curator, Christian Thomsen who had trouble displaying the artifacts his museum held.[74]

Mr. Thomsen held that the items that came from graves only containing stone were from an earlier era than those graves holding only Bronze artifacts and iron came after all three. His theory was upheld by further research, although those works were based upon the assumption that Thomsen was correct.[75]

While there may have been some confirmation of this thinking it is not without its errors. One being the assumptions that all people of all ancient societies behaved as Mr. Thomsen and subsequent archaeologists had stated.

The three-age system is vulnerable to misidentification because so little is known about what the occupant of the grave and his family, etc. did and owned in their lifetime.

Dating the past is a very subjective task as the archaeologist usually does not have any written contemporary documentation to explain the find.

A lot of educated guesswork is involved and the same can be said of the confirmation excavations that were carried out after Mr. Thomsen created this theory.[76]

There is another problem with the three-age system. It works only in Europe and the Mediterranean. The reasoning behind this non universal application is that some societies skipped different stages. It is also due to the fact that colonial rulers and then later independent nationalism would distort the history of a given nation.[77]

The key item that needs to be remembered here is that the origin of the three-age system was human. Secular human at that and was solely based on arbitrary and very subjective thinking. It was not based on actual fact or even the truth.[78]

The creator of the system and his fellow supporters did not let the Bible influence their thinking and totally ignored Genesis 4:22, which reads

As for Zillah, she also gave birth to Tubal-cain, the forger of all implements of bronze and iron; and the sister of Tubal-cain was Naamah. (NASB)

Tubal-cain's birth was the 6th generation after Cain and the 7th after Adam. This means that prior to his birth Adam and his family used stone tools to handle their cultivation of fruits, vegetables and tending to their flocks or herds.

The time frame for this advancement may have been as short as 250 years if we use the number 40 for each generation. Or it could have been a bit longer.

What this information does is throw off Mr. Thomsen's conclusions about the 3 Age system. Bronze and iron were around a lot longer than he or any secular archaeologist gives them credit.

This is why Christians, including Christian archaeologists and scholars cannot go along with secular conclusions. God has given us different information that is true. After all, he was there and saw it all take place.

Whereas the later museum curators, archaeologists and bible scholars were not. The later professionals can only guess when a grave site was dug and used.

They can only guess at the reasoning behind why such graves held only stone tools while others housed metal ones.

The financial state of the occupant is rarely included in the thinking of archaeologists when examining these tombs.

It is highly possible that the occupant did not have the money needed to purchase the expensive tools or that he or she made a request to be buried with only stone, etc., because those implements held special meaning to the person in the grave.

We cannot assume that the experts have made a positive identification with so many assumptions being used to date the different ages.

Then, it is also possible that the stone tool holding graves did have bronze and iron artifacts inside of them.

Since metal is vulnerable to outside destructive forces, they could have decayed and disappeared faster in some graves than in others. It all depends on the conditions surrounding the graves.[79]

These are factors left out of the research conducted that helped confirm Mr. Thomsen's creation of the three-age system.

Finally, because societies develop at different rates, what is labeled stone age may have been a part of the iron age or bronze age and so on.

The presence of stone age tribes in the 20th and 21st century show that dating the ages is not exact and open to error.

Who Owns Archaeology

This can be a difficult question to answer. A lot will depend on the country a person lives in and the type of government that nation has ruling over it.

Many countries, especially in the Middle East, have established their own antiquities arm of the government. For Israel it is the IAA, or the Israel Antiquities Authority, and it is charged with the responsibility to oversee excavations and other archaeological matters.[80]

They are not the only country that has an established antiquities organization that controls archaeological work within its boundaries. Egypt has what is called the Supreme Council of Antiquities and they can rule the history of Egypt with an iron hand.[81]

With that authority what is uncovered usually belongs to the state. Artifacts, manuscripts, and even buildings are owned by the country they were uncovered in, making sure that they are well cared for, protected and available to scholars and others.

This is not the case for every country though. For some, the people who own the discovered physical remains depends on who owns the property the artifact, etc., was found on. Of course, limitations have been set over the years and the Treasure Act of 1996 is just one example of the type of restrictions that come into play. This act governs archaeology work in Britain and the rest of the United Kingdom.[82]

Then there is the case of those early discoveries that were uncovered by different explorers often called treasure hunters. These men and women often worked for museums who sent them into the Middle East and other countries in hopes of making discoveries that would make the museum famous.[83]

Archaeology may only have been formed in the late 1700s yet many of the uncovered treasures were sent back to the home country, long before any discussion on ethics, acquisition and ownership started to take place. In other words, possession is 9/10ths of the law seemed to prevail win the world of archaeology until different nations began to form their own antiquities organizations.[84]

There can still be some argument today over different archaeological pieces that are discovered.

Nations certainly have the right to impose ownership over their history even if that history is from a different ancient nation from the modern one that resides on the same land.

There are some ownership advocates who go as far as saying that it is the dead or their descendants who truly own a grave and that archaeologists are violating the rights of those owners when they start to excavate a grave. In their minds those graves if no family can be found rightfully belong to the state not the investigating archaeologist.[85]

This argument probably will never be solved to anyone's satisfaction. But the real question in this debate is who owns the narrative that is created by the different archaeological discoveries?

If you are familiar with the research field you should be aware that any ancient manuscript or artifact, etc., spawns about 5 different narratives.

That reality should tell you that no one really owns the narrative. The narrative is at the mercy of the archaeologist, bible scholar or armchair archaeologist who looks at the information surrounding the discovery.

They then spin their own narrative, often disagreeing with each other what the discovery means. This battle is seen in Eilat Mazar's identification of the palace of David she feels she has found after years of searching.[86]

Because the narrative of the past is not owned by anyone or any state, everyone is free to form their own opinions using the physical evidence that has been published as they see fit.

In archaeology itself, there is no real set of ethical rules that governs the use of the uncovered artifacts.

That use depends on the moral character of the person doing the construction of the narrative. Those who do not hold to a biblical standard of morality or right and wrong, tend to be freer with their narratives.

The believers are under the restriction of God's word and they must be honest, truthful and make sure they do not fudge any data to make their narrative fit their agenda or purpose.

For those who merely read about archaeology, they must be able to discern between truth and lies in order to find the right narrative that provides the correct picture of the past.

Nothing is New Under the Sun

The modern world is not always history literate. Many times over, an ad pops up declaring that a new invention is being introduced to the world.

Little thought is given to what Solomon said in the book of Ecclesiastes 1 when these new inventions are introduced to the world.

He wrote about 3,000 years ago the following words:

> That which has been is that which will be,
> And that which has been done is that which will be done.
> So there is nothing new under the sun (Ecc. 1:9 NASB)

When someone starts looking at history, one can see the truth in those words. There is very little that is thought of today that has not been thought of in the past.

One example is air travel. While the ancients may not have had the tools and raw resources to produce aircraft, they still had birds.

Thinking about how easy traveling by air would be is not something that started with the Wright Brothers.

But there are other modern inventions that have ancient roots. One example is the K cup. This is a modern single serving coffee cup for people who need speed, convenience and less of a mess to cleanup. But it is not a new concept as the British Museum holds a Minoan single serve cup in its exhibits, the idea for convenience came about 3,500 years ago.[87]

Weapons of war were not new when some were invented during the Middle Ages or improved upon in the modern age. They have been a staple of battles since at least the ancient Greek times. Archimedes invented catapults and stone throwing machines as well as other ship destroying weapons. While the catapult enjoyed long lasting success, the others were mere inspiration for more modern weapons.[88]

Then there is what is known as the ancient Greek computer. The Antikythera mechanism was discovered in 1900 and has shown the world that the ancient world knew about gears, complex design and mechanical knowledge. It also showed that the ancient people knew about astronomy as this mechanism was used to track eclipses, the stars and more. It is said to have been made in about 205 BC but not by Archimedes.[89]

But contrary to popular opinion by archaeologists and scholars, the ancient Greeks were not the inventors of the many inventions they were credited with.

Many came long before their time and the possible reason the Greeks are credited with inventing everything is that Alexander and his armies conquered the known world.

It would have been easy for him and his people to take credit for other people's work. One example is the Pythagorean Theorem.

It has been said for centuries that Pythagoras of Samos who lived in the 6th century BC is credited with coming up with his famous theory. Yet, he was not the first. Who came up with the theory originally is not known but it was used by both the Babylonians and the ancient Chinese 1,000 years before Pythagoras used it.[90]

Staying with the Babylonians the modern world is not the inventor of the Social Security system. That idea was used by the old Babylonian governments to help their elderly citizens make it through the later years of their lives. Also, time capsules were used by the ancient Babylonians to give future societies a glimpse into their lifestyles and society.[91]

The womanly desire to look beautiful did not start in the 18th, 19th or even the 20th century AD.

As long as there have been women on this planet, the desire for them to change their looks through using make up has been around Egyptian women as far back as 4,000 BC were using eye shadow to capture the attention and hearts of men. The only difference between their make-up and modern versions is that the Egyptian cosmetic industry did not use chemicals in their concoctions.[92]

Then there were the Romans. While they did not invent the arch that created some very long lasting and very durable aqueducts, they have been credited with inventing concrete. Modern scientists like to think of this concrete as inferior to the modern version, but the Roman made concrete has lasted for thousands of years in structures like the Colosseum. It was some very tough construction material.[93]

There are some honorable mentions that should be included in this chapter. Chocolate was invented about1000 BC, zero was used first in about 300 BC by the Sumerians and Babylonians while the Maya used it in about 350 AD. Newspapers were thought of about 2200 years ago and were used like today to spread the important news of the day. Everyone knows of the story of the Marathon. This race celebrates the achievement of one Athenian soldier who ran 26 miles to spread the good news that the Athenians beat the Persians at the Battle of Marathon[94]

This list of ancient inventions is not a closed list. It covers almost every aspect of life including astronomy. The lenses for telescopes and glasses go back long before Galileo used a telescope. The ancient Minoans were known to have telescope type lenses back in about 1400 BC and earlier.[95]

When one does a comprehensive investigation, they would be amazed at how the ancients beat the modern world in sophistication, accuracy, and use.

Even medical surgery and construction of buildings are not left out as archaeologists have uncovered pieces of evidence showing how good the ancients were at both industries.

In spite of what evolutionists and other scientists claim the ancient world was like. The reality is that the ancients were far ahead of their time.

They were not knuckle dragging cave dwelling idiots afraid of fire. They were people given the same God given intellect, talents, and capabilities that God has endowed the modern people with.

If nothing was new in Solomon's day, think about how few inventions are new today. Even the concept of electricity and batteries has ancient roots. We may not know the full extent of the knowledge and use of those items the ancients had. But one thing is for sure, nothing is new under the sun even today.

The Amount of Biblical Evidence

What a lot of unbelievers, whether they be archaeologists, bible scholars or common people, do not want you to know is that there is an enormous amount of archaeological evidence supporting the Bible.

It is impossible to list all of what has been uncovered here in this little chapter, but enough examples will be given to let you know how true the Bible is and how archaeology supports its record.

One of the first major pieces of evidence for the Bible and the people mentioned in it, is the verification of about 50 people found in archaeological discoveries. Their names have been found in a variety of places including inscriptions written in the same time period mentioned in the Bible. They are not all Hebrew people either.[96]

The following list is all taken from one source and will be footnoted at the end of the list:

#1. Nebo-Sarsekim—The British museum unveiled a clay tablet that references a court official of King Nebuchadnezzar found in the Book of Jeremiah.2 The cuneiform inscription translates as Nebo-Sarsekim and is dated to around 595 BC.

#2. Seal of Jezebel—Dutch researcher Marjo Korpel presented a strong case for having identified the official seal of the wicked Queen Jezebel on an opal signet.6 Korpel's work seems to confirm the suspicions of the late pioneering archaeologist, Nahman Avigad, who believed the royal seal belonged to Jezebel, a name documented nowhere outside the Old Testament.

#3. Beehives—Amihai Mazar, Professor of Archaeology at the Hebrew University, revealed the first beehive colony, dating to the biblical era, has been excavated at Tel Rehov, Israel.8 Dating from the 9th to 10th centuries BC, it is the earliest known beehive colony in the archaeological record. In sixteen different places, the Bible describes Israel as the 'land of milk and honey'. And more specifically, Judges 14:8–9 describes how Samson took bee honey from inside the carcass of a lion and 1 Samuel 14:27 describes how Jonathan, King Saul's son, dipped his hand into a honeycomb during a battle

#4. Excavations at Nuzi (1925-41), Mari (discovered in 1933), and Alalakh (1937-39; 1946-49) provide helpful background information that fits well with the Genesis stories of the patriarchal period. The Nuzi tablets and Mari letters illustrate the patriarchal customs in great detail, and the Ras Shamra tablets discovered in ancient Ugarit in Syria shed much light on Hebrew prose and poetry and Canaanite culture. The Ebla tablets discovered recently in northern Syria also affirm the antiquity and accuracy of the Book of Genesis

#5. Revolt of Moab against Israel (2 Kings 1:1; 3:4-27), recorded on the Mesha Inscription.

Fall of Samaria (2 Kings 17:3-6, 24; 18:9-11) to Sargon II, king of Assyria, as recorded on his palace walls.

Defeat of Ashdod by Sargon II (Isaiah 20:1), as recorded on his palace walls

#6. The Hittites were once thought to be a Biblical legend, until their capital and records were discovered at Bogazkoy, Turkey

-Another king who was in doubt was Belshazzar, king of Babylon, named in Daniel 5. The last king of Babylon was Nabonidus according to recorded history. Tablets were found showing that Belshazzar was Nabonidus' son who served as coregent in Babylon. Thus, Belshazzar could offer to make Daniel "third highest ruler in the kingdom" (Dan. 5:16) for reading the handwriting on the wall, the highest available position. Here we see the "eye-witness" nature of the Biblical record, as is so often brought out by the discoveries of archaeology.

#7. The pool of Gibeon where the forces of David and Ish-bosheth fought during the struggle for the kingship of Israel (2 Samuel 2:12-32).

-The Pool of Heshbon, likened to the eyes of the Shulammite woman (Song of Songs 7:4).

#8. The royal palace at Samaria where the kings of Israel lived (1 Kings 20:43; 21:1, 2; 22:39; 2 Kings 1:2; 15:25).

-The Pool of Samaria where King Ahab's chariot was washed after his death (1 Kings 22:29-38).

-The water tunnel beneath Jerusalem dug by King Hezekiah to provide water during the Assyrian siege (2 Kings 20:20; 2 Chronicles 32:30).

-The royal palace in Babylon where King Belshazzar held the feast and Daniel interpreted the handwriting on the wall (Daniel 5)

-The royal palace in Susa where Esther was queen of the Persian king Xerxes (Esther 1:2; 2:3, 5, 9, 16).

-The royal gate at Susa where Mordecai, Esther's cousin, sat (Esther 2:19, 21; 3:2, 3; 4:2; 5:9, 13; 6:10, 12).

-The Square in front of the royal gate at Susa where Mordecai met with Halthach, Xerxes' eunuch (Esther 4:6).

#9. The following is a record of a census taken in the year 104 A.D. which contains similar wording to that found in the Gospel: "From the Prefect of Egypt, Gaius Vibius Maximus. Being that the time has come for the house to house census, it is mandatory that all men who are living outside of their districts return to their own homelands, that the census may be carried out."

#10 In 1975, a collection of nearly 250 clay seals were found about 44 miles southwest of Jerusalem. These small lumps of clay that are impressed with a seal, in ancient times served as an official signature for an individual. The clay seals were then attached to documents to identify the sender. Amazingly, among the seals that were found were the names of three Biblical figures mentioned in the 36th chapter of the book of Jeremiah.

The first clay seal is impressed with the following inscription: Berekhyahu son of Neriyahu the scribe

-A second clay seal has been found that was impressed with the name of the scribe Elishama. It reads as follows: 'Elishama' servant of the king. According to the Bible, Elishama was a scribe who served the king. He is recorded in Jeremiah 36:10-12[97]

As you can see the list is a bit endless. They also do not contain the over 5,000 New testament manuscripts that have been uncovered through archaeological work. Nor the hundreds more that are readily available to be examined at different museums around the world.

There is probably more evidence for biblical figures, events, people and civilizations than any other people group or secular text.

Take some time and research to see how much evidence archaeology has uncovered that supports the biblical record.

Does Archaeology Prove the Bible True

This can be a contentious question to try and answer. As seen in the previous chapter, archaeology certainly has turned up a wealth of physical evidence showing that the Bible is grounded in history, in the actual eras each book was written and so on.

The Dead Sea Scrolls may not testify to the truthfulness of the biblical record, but they go a long way to show that the Bible has remained unaltered for 2,000 years.

For many believers, the answer to the above question is that yes, archaeology does prove the Bible true.

Yet, not all believers or even archaeologists and scholars would go that far and make such a definitive positive statement about archaeology's support for the Bible.

F.F. Bruce did not like the word confirmation and went as far as to say that archaeology supplied illustrative evidence to support the biblical record. He goes on to say that archaeology supplies the necessary background to help frame the New testament solidly in the 1st century and demonstrates that its ac-counts do not fit later centuries.[98]

People may not like the word prove when they talk about bib-lical evidence and prefer to use the term confirm or confirma-tion. But confirming something is the exact same thing as prov-ing something true. Confirmation is verification and when you have verification then you know something is true.[99]

Despite what the scholars and archaeologists say, archaeology tends to prove the Bible true continuously.

You can tap dance around the issue by using words like 'affirm' but that term also means to validate something or to maintain something as true. The term affirm comes with the same defin-ition as the terms 'confirm' and 'prove'.[100]

There is no getting around the fact that archaeology does prove the Bible true. One thing that should be kept in mind is that the physical evidence unearthed by archaeology does not create faith. The person who is doubting the Bible still needs to take that step of faith and believe that the evidence is correct, and that the Bible is true.[101]

Also, while we have more than enough physical evidence to show that the Bible is true, there will not be physical evidence for many of the events recorded in the Bible.

For example, we cannot find the jawbone of the ass Samson used to attack the Philistines. There would be too many lying around Israel to be able to distinguish which one he used. There will only be enough physical evidence to support one's Christian faith.

That does not mean that those events lacking physical evidence are untrue. The amount of physical evidence supporting the biblical record speaks for those other events as well.

For the Bible to be God's word, it must be true in all parts of it from Genesis to Revelation.

This fact does not stop unbelievers from demanding physical evidence for every page of the Bible.

They also demand scientific evidence to show that science and its theories about the Bible and our origins are wrong.

The problem is that these same unbelievers dismiss the host of physical evidence the scientific field of archaeology has uncovered that proves the Bible true.

You can find different types of evidence that prove beyond a shadow of a doubt that the Bible is true and there will still be those professionals and other unbelievers who will find some fault with it and reject it as evidence.

Belief is done by making a choice whether there is evidence or not. The believer does not need to have physical evidence to show the Bible is true.

They just have to have faith and believe God and his word. That is it. Believing God is showing faith and that act pleases him.

The Anti Biblical Bias in Archaeology

Objectivity is not the only real problem that Christian archaeologists face when uncovering the past.

There is a great anti biblical bias that permeates the field that is hard to overcome. Many archaeologists and even biblical scholars do not view the Bible in a favorable light. Instead, they see the Bible as religious writings that has no scientific, teaching or archaeological value.[102]

There are many different reasons for this anti biblical bias. Unfortunately, there are enough academics that hold to this view who pass on their bias to their students. The exclusion of the Bible is not held by every professional archaeologist but there are enough of them to make a negative impact on biblical archaeology's purpose and work.[103]

This is not a new phenomenon. While the 18th and early 19th centuries held the Bible in high esteem, things began to change for archaeology in the later years of the 19th when Darwin's Origins of the Species and other works were published and became popular.[104]

Just before the 20th century began Ernst Troeltsch, followed by Rudolph Bultmann and Albert Schweitzer in the early 20th centuries all published works that helped influence biblical scholars and archaeologists. Those works challenged the biblical views held by at the time mainstream archaeologists and scholars. Those authors preferred science to the bible, wanted to demythologize the New Testament and tried to separate Jesus in to 2 categories, the Jesus of history and the Jesus of theology.[105]

In more recent times Israeli archaeologist I. Finkelstein and his co-author N.A. Silberman published a book that down graded both David and Solomon to mere chieftains, if they existed at all. They took the approach that the stories about both early kings of Israel had their achievements read into their lives and that the Bible embellished their stories for some patriotic reason. They used the limited and inferior field of archaeology to make their point without really compensating for those limitations and destructive elements that hinder archaeological research.[106]

Part of their justification for their conclusions was that neither king received much extra biblical attention as the two authors would have liked to have seen. Their view is that the biblical authors exaggerated the accounts as archaeological discoveries fail to produce the physical evidence that would normally substantiate the accounts.[107]

One of the best examples for anti-bible bias is the Copenhagen School of Thought or commonly known as the minimalists. This group of people reject much of the biblical record simply because archaeology does not support what the Bible has recorded. When presented with actual physical evidence, the minimalists seek long and hard to find ways to refute and reject that evidence presented to them.[108]

One of the more well-known minimalists is the late Philip Davies. He is known to reject actual and verifiable physical evidence without even entertaining one iota of the data with an open mind. He is also known for trying to separate the Hebrew people of history from the Hebrew people recorded in the Bible. The foundation for this type of thinking is based more on what has not been found than what has been found. It is also very arbitrary classification that has its origin in the bias against the Bible which Mr. Davies held.[109]

This archaeological bias, found in too many bible scholars and archaeologist, then influences on how the Bible is read. It is taken more as a document for religious and theological purposes and not a historical text that can be of use today.

The contents in the Bible are seen as fairy tales meant to oppress and enslave anyone living in ancient Israel and beyond.

Those anti bible professionals have a variety of ways at looking at the ancient people of Israel, none of which really coincides with the biblical record, even though those views point to different passages of scripture.[110]

What this reading of scripture does is not undermine the biblical record but shows that these scholars and archaeologists do not understand the Bible.

It also shows that they do not know how to read the Bible as they place their personal anti believing bias on the Bible's contents.

To get to the truth about the Bible's contents and our past is a difficult journey especially when there is so much anti biblical bias flowing through the archaeological world.

It gets harder and harder to know whom to believe especially when fanatical believers and pseudo-archaeologists add their voices to the mix.

But it is not an impossible task as Jesus told us we would know the truth. The key is not to assume that everyone declaring they are Christian are telling the truth.

Unbelievers are easier to ignore and dismiss as their words are not coming with the help of God.

To get to the truth one must ignore what the unbeliever says and rely on both the Bible and the physical evidence discovered.

We do not toss the evidence out just because an unbelieving archaeologist or biblical scholar has discovered it.

We use it and follow the Spirit of Truth to the truth.

The Bible is a Reliable Ancient Text

Despite the anti-bible bias in archaeology, it is still possible to see the reliability of the text.

It is not the Bible that is limited in its scope. As seen earlier, archaeology has too many limitations to appoint it judge and jury over the contents of the Bible.

Also, archaeologists are only human. Their view of the past is extremely limited as well. They can only see the past through what manuscripts, artifacts and buildings, etc., that have been discovered.

In a most cases, the physical evidence excavated bring a very blurry and disjointed picture of the past. These discoveries do not present the whole story, leaving archaeologists to make educated guesses about what those discoveries represent.

On the other hand, the Bible is not so limited. The books were written by God who was and is the only eyewitness still alive who witnessed all of the events mentioned in the Bible.

The men God used were present at those events as well. We know this because of the extensive extra biblical manuscript discoveries that show that the names etc. Used for people and locations in the Bible are in their correct era.[111]

But that is not all, Jericho has long been a thorn in the bible believer's side. When Kathleen Kenyon contradicted Dr. Garstang and declared Jericho uninhabited at the time of the Exodus and beginning of the Conquest, many archaeologists leapt on this bandwagon and declared the Bible unreliable. Sadly, her conclusions came from what she did not find. They also were accepted even though she never published her final report on her excavations.[112]

Dr. Bryant Wood did another examination of all the evidence and reports available for Jericho and found many other interesting pieces of physical evidence that shed more light on the archaeological site and showed that Ms.Kenyon made some errors in judgment. One of those pieces of evidence discovered was that the walls fell exactly like the Bible said, with a portion of the wall remaining intact.[113]

These are not the only discoveries that help prove the Bible as a reliable ancient text. If you recall the trouble the Hittites caused when for over 1800 years the Bible was the only ancient text to mention their name. 1906 saw the discovery of a 10,000 clay tablet library that helped prove the existence of these people.[114]

Some people claim that the biblical writers were referring to a mythological kingdom but that is far from the truth. Others wonder how the Hittites lived in Canaan in Abraham's time. Like today, the ancient world was full of people moving from one nation to another for whatever reason they had.[115]

There are scholars that point to the presence of camels in Lot's and Abraham's herds as evidence that the Bible is unreliable.[116]

But there are a lot of errors in that conclusion. The earliest discovery of camels may not be in Abraham's time but those remains do into indicate when camels first entered Canaan.

They are just the earliest to date discoveries of the existence of camels. There is nothing that prevented either Lot or Abraham from bringing camels into the promised land from Ur.

To find the earliest use of camels, archaeologists should be digging in Abraham's original country not Israel.

Thus, the bible is not in error here. The anti-biblical bias influences those wrong conclusions about the camels and the biblical record.

Carbon dating is not much help here either. That dating method can only date the remains analyzed. It cannot produce a figure that states when camels originally entered the land. To use that dating system to uphold an anti-biblical opinion is not using the dating tool wisely but using it to manipulate professional and public opinion towards a pre-determined conclusion.[117]

It is not archaeology that is claiming that the Bible is unreliable. What is trying to undermine the biblical record is the anti-biblical bias that is held by unbelieving archaeologists, bible scholars and teachers.

Archaeology continues to confirm the biblical reliability over and over. There are a myriad of discoveries that overwhelm that one about camels and other dissenting views.[118]

Why We Study History

The information for this chapter and the next one are taken from the author's published articles found HubPages and at the following link https://hubpages.com/@davidtee under the same name)

History and archaeology may not be as exciting as a professional football or basketball game, but it is probably more important than watching millionaires running up and down the field/court of play.

There are a lot of reasons why we should study history and this chapter will outline those reasons for you.

The study of both history and archaeology is important for believers to remain strong believers. That study helps them finish their race.

Here is a list of reasons why all believers should do some historical study:

- God wants us to study- he says so in I Timothy. He wants knowledgeable followers not ignorant ones

• We get to the truth- studying history and archae-ology is but one way to get to some truth. It is not the only way and they do not hold all truth

• We learn that many cultic beliefs are not new but have ancient foundations

• We get information on how to refute cultic and other false religious beliefs

• We get respect from unbelievers- this is because we actually know something. One of the biggest complaints from atheists is that Christians do not know the Bible or their history

• We get information to refute other unbelievers and their alternative theories

• We learn that the secular experts are not telling the truth

• We protect our faith- too many unwary and un-prepared young believers lose their faith when they encounter those unbelieving professors who do not believe in God, accept that he exists, or believe the Bible

• We learn that the Bible is correct and that the sec-ular experts, professors, etc., do not know more than God

• We learn how to follow the Holy Spirit to the truth (John 16:13)

How Should Believers Study History & Archaeology

The how to is as important as the study. This is for the simple reason that believers can be sidetracked by evil and go off in the wrong direction.

If this happens then they would be like the evolutionist looking for the truth by going down the wrong paths and looking in the wrong places for their answers.

Here are some steps in how to study history and archaeology

• Ask God for help- you will not get to the truth by excluding the one who holds all truth

• Follow biblical instructions- Psalm 1 is one big key- do not follow the unbeliever or their counsel. Another is found in Ecc.- nothing is new under the sun.

• Read good books- we wrote on this recently. You will not find all the information you need in Christian books. You will have to read good secular works to get all the evidence and information you need. You will need God to help you not stray into adopting the secular theories or ideas.

• Remember that the bible contains actual history- there has never been a historical or archaeological discovery yet that proves the Bible wrong or disagrees with the Bible. What disagrees with the Bible is the archaeologists' theories, assumptions, leaps to conclusions, speculation and so on.

• Remember that God does not lie, and the Bible is not wrong- the people who lie are those who do not believe in God or follow him

• Read the church fathers and other ancient writers- but again remember that they were human and may not have all the answers even though they lived earlier in history.

• Stick to the truth- never stray from it. Once you find the truth, adopt it, keep it and adapt your life accordingly. Even in your discussions with unbelievers, do not stray from the truth

• Remember that the secular way is not God's way- this includes the secular scientific method. Archaeologists want believers to be objective but that is impossible. There is no gray middle ground. The secular scientific method only looks for the best explanation NOT the truth. There is a difference.

• Learn the different schools of thought and why they are wrong or right- Minimalist sometimes sound like the believe the Bible but they reject most of the OT.

• Learn the difference between credible archaeologists and bad ones- this includes bible scholars, historians and so on.

Why We Study History 2

One of the most important reasons comes from Jesus' own words to Peter when they had finished breakfast.

John 21:15 - 17 records Jesus' admonition to Peter to feed his sheep. He stressed how important it was to provide the right spiritual food to those who believe in Jesus.

Studying history and archaeology helps pastors, missionaries, Sunday school teachers and parents find the right food to feed the followers of Christ.

The problem with some church leaders is that they do not have the right information to pass on to their charges.

Or they spend too much time repeating the gospel message to the very ones who have already heard and accepted it.

This tactic does not build strong warriors for Christ., Instead, it leaves the people of God vulnerable to evil and its minions.

Unbelievers do a lot of studying of history and have been able to trick believers into thinking the Bible is not true.

That situation is not pleasing to God. As the Bible states we are to get knowledge, wisdom and understanding.

Believers also need to learn how to do good research if they are going to be successful in refuting unbelievers' arguments against the Bible.

Not only that, they must be able to know what is the truth, and present that truth in a honest way. It is a shame when popular Christian authors do worse scholarship than the unbelieving authors.

A musical choir director does not have the choir sing 'Jesus Loves Me' in every service and expects them to grow as a choir or expand their musical talents.

He provides direction, information and more difficult pieces to achieve that goal. So must the church leader. They have to take their people past square one, the gospel, and move them on to more difficult information to make sure they grow and are equipped so God can use them.

Different church leaders complain about the many youth in their churches that are leaving their faith.

One reason for this is that they were not taught the right information nor given the right historical information to keep their faith strong.

The Bible and Christians are not the originators of the flat earth concept that unbelievers accuse them of. With the right training and information, believers would learn that concept originated with the ancient Greek scientists.

The book Aristarchus of Samos: The Ancient Copernicus by Sir Thomas Heath outlines how that belief got started. The Bible never teaches that the earth is flat.

What the Bible does do is use certain terms that have been in use for hundreds, if not thousands of years.

Those terms are used to make sure everyone understands what is being said in the biblical passage.

Also, when presented with the correct information, the people of the church, both young and old, can stand strong realizing that the ancient societies and man were just like them.

They were intelligent, creative, innovative and more. The modern believer would also learn that the ancients were not knuckle dragging animals that lived in caves and were afraid of fire.

They will see that God made ancient man exactly like he made modern man. In studying history believers get the answers they are looking.

In the biblical pages we find out information that secular science cannot uncover.

Topics like the origins of many, languages, different nations, and other important topics are made clear in the Bible, while science is still stumbling around in the dark.

Getting the right information, understanding it and then following God's lead in how to dispense that knowledge to the people is of the utmost importance.

Building up God's people so that they are strong in the truth and their faith is the pastors', etc., duty.

Finally, studying history shows the believer where the unbeliever is wrong. It also gives us tools to fight off the unbeliever's ideas and keep them honest.

Without knowledgeable properly trained believers in history and archaeology, the unbeliever has carte blanche in creating any scenario about the past they want to have.

The believer needs to point out the unbelievers' errors and produce the evidence, etc. To support their arguments. It is the only way to keep the lies of the unbelieving world away from the public.

Studying history is a very important tool for the believers to learn and wield correctly.

Some Final Words

The world of archaeology is not as romantic as the movies portray. There is no swashbuckling hero who wields a gun and a whip to reach artifact treasure.

Instead some were spies using a legitimate archaeological organization as a cover.[119] But for the most part, archaeology is used by normal people to investigate the past while digging up ancient artifacts, buildings and more.

As you can see, there is a lot more to the field of archaeology than meets the eye. Most archaeologists and supporters of that research field like people to think it is a very scientific research field that uncovers the truth.

Unfortunately, that is not always the case especially when the Bible is involved. The bias against the biblical record is not a hidden secret.

This bias tends to confuse those who only see the surface, the major articles that describe the latest discovery.

Underneath, there is a little war going on as there are explorers who try really hard to prove that the Bible is nothing but a book full of myths.

These people use assumption, leaps to conclusions, conjecture and hypothesis to build their case.

Most often these arguments can be refuted because those con-clusions are often based on what is not found and not on what has been found.

Kathleen Kenyon's opinion about Jericho and the Hebrew con-quest is a prime example of those errors.

Kenneth Kitchen disposed of those arguments with his famous 'absence of evidence is not evidence for absence' motto that has inspired many a modern archaeologist to continue on and not give up when physical evidence remains out of reach.[120]

Just because we cannot find a particular piece of physical evi-dence, a n ancient civilization and so on does not mean that the Bible is wrong.

But that is the automatic conclusion that unbelievers leap to when nothing is found. The reason for the lack of evidence is many fold.

The archaeologists could have been digging in the wrong place, have not gone deep enough or a natural disaster, war, or construction has wiped it from existence.

There is so much that can go wrong in the pursuit of physical remains that enlighten the world about humanity's past.

For believers we cannot put our hope in archaeology. As some archaeologists have found out the limitations of the research field have damaged enough people's Christian faith when that is done.

Believers do not need physical evidence to believe God and his word. It does help when we get some, but archaeological confirmation is not necessary.

We believe God like little children believe their parents. His word is enough. When bits and pieces are uncovered then all archaeology does is strengthen that belief.

In the 250+ years that archaeology has been professionally conducted, there has never been an archaeological discovery proving the Bible wrong.

What that tells us is that the real source for opposition to the Bible comes from evil as it deceives those who do not believe God.

Archaeology is a dual edged sword, where discoveries build up faith, and the lack of discoveries tear that faith down.

Believers can never be in the latter group if they decide to take God's word over archaeology's conclusions.

The one question that has never received an answer whenever it is asked is "Where in the Bible do both God and Jesus say to take science and its word over their words?"

Archaeology may be a scientific research field but like all other sciences, it does not trump God and the Bible.

It is too limited, cannot resurrect lost manuscripts or artifacts, and more. Plus, a majority of the practicing archaeologists, bible scholars and teachers do not believe God nor follow the Spirit of Truth to the truth.

The believer must hold to God and his word first and foremost if they are going to run their race and finish it favorably.

Archaeology is only a tool that helps us understand the Bible better and see that God's word is not a book of fables.

God does not lie nor does he have hidden agendas. He just wants us to take him at his word.

About the Author

Dr. David Tee was a teacher in Korea for 14 years, teaching English throughout the country. During that time he continued his studies and added to his BTH a Masters of Ministry in History and Archaeology, A Masters of Biblical Archaeology and a Doctor of Theology.

While doing this and teaching he found time to write on a variety of topics that were published in the Korea Times. Along with that writing, he wrote his own blog www.theologyarchaeology.wordpress.com

Books by the Author

Archaeology: What You need to know
    Archaeology & the Unwary Believer
    Much to Talk About Vols. 1 & 2

---

[1] Law, S., 2019 Huge Hidden Older City Emerges from Under Biblical City of Gath https://patternsofevidence.com/2019/08/02/hidden-city-emerges-from-under-biblical-gath/

[2] Kitchen, K, The Bible in its World pages 10ff

[3] Janeway, B 2006 Relearning Old Lessons: Archaeologists Fail to Use Sound

Reasoning, Associates for Biblical Research

[4] Calder, AQ 2007 Losing faith: how secular scholarship affects scholars   https://creation.com/losing-faith-how-secular-scholarship-affects-scholars

[5] Calder, AQ 2007

[6] Janeway, B 2006

[7] Titus 1:2 NASB

[8] Mirriam Webster Dictionary 2019 https://www.merriam-webster.com/dictionary/archaeology

[9] Miller II, RD, 2011, Once More: Minimalism, Maximalism, and Objectivity http://www.bibleinterp.com/opeds/miller358004.shtml

[10] Matthew 6:24 NASB

[11] Dever, Wm., Did God Have a Wife pgs. ix & 82 Eerdmans

[12] Ibid, pg. 73

[13] Finkelstein I, et al, 2007 Has King David's Palace in Jerusalem been found, Tel Aviv

[14] Borowski, O., 1982 Digging, Dug Gone BAR 8:1 January February

[15] Battle Over Bones, BAR 23:06 Nov./Dec. 1997

[16] Seiglie, M., 2003, The Exodus Controversy Bible & Spade 16:2, Spring pg. 34ff

[17] Ibid

[18] Kitchen, KA., 2003, On the Reliability of the Old Testament Eerdmans pg. 466

[19] Kitchen, KA., The Bible in Its World, ch. 1

[20] Lichocka, B., Forgery on the Nile Research for Mediterreanean Archaeology, Warsaw Academy of Science zaspan@zaspan.waw.pl

[21] Cargill, R., First person: Introducing the new BAR, BAR, January/February 2020

[22] Yardeni, A., Hershel's Crusade, No. 3: Forgeries and Unprovenanced Artifacts BAR, 44:2 March, April , MAy, June 2018

[23] Shanks, H., 2007, Special Report Jerusalem Forgery Conference Biblical Archaeology Society www.biblicalarchaeology.org[1]

[24] Shanks, H., 2007

[25] Ibid

[26] Cargill, R., 2018, The Importance of Archaeological Provenance – BAR Sept/Oct 2018, The Official Blog of Dr. Robert Cargill, https://robertcargill.com/2018/09/21/the-importance-of-archaeological-provenance/

[27] IBid

[28] Shanks, H., 2007

[29] Cargill, R., Sept. 2018

[30] Cline, E., 2007, Raiders of the Faux Ark, Boston Globe http://archive.boston.com/news/globe/ideas/articles/2007/09/30/raiders_of_the_faux_ark/

[31] Cline, E., 2007

[32] The Discovery of the Rosetta Stone Biblical Archaeology 2019 https://www.bible-history.com/links.php?cat=36&sub=5030&cat_name=Biblical+Archaeology&sub-cat_name=The+Rosetta+Stone

[33] BAS Staff, 2011, Bible Artifacts Found Outside the Trench: The Amarna Tablets https://www.biblicalarchaeology.org/daily/biblical-artifacts/artifacts-and-the-bible/bible-artifacts-found-outside-the-trench-the-amarna-tablets/

[34] BAS Staff, 2011

[35] Meyer, M., 2018, The Gnostic Discoveries: The Impact of the Nag Hammadi Library https://www.catholicireland.net/the-gnostic-discoveries-the-impact-of-the-nag-hammadi-library/

[36] Varner, W., 2008, What is the importance of the Dead Sea Scrolls Associates for Biblical Research https://biblearchaeology.org/research/founder-s-corner/3590-What-is-the-importance-of-the-Dead-Sea-Scrolls

---

[37] Wood, BG, 2011,The Tel Dan Stela and the Kings of Aram and Israel Associates for Biblical research https://biblearchaeology.org/research/contemporary-issues/2233-the-tel-dan-stela-and-the-kings-of-aram-and-israel?highlight=WyJ0ZWwiLCIndGVsIiwidGVsJ3MiLCJkYW4iLCJzdFx1MDBlOGxlIiwic3RlbGUncyIsInN0ZWxlJ3NmaXJzdCIsImRpc2NvdmVyeSIsIidka XNjb3ZlcnkiLCJnZGlzY292ZXJ5JyIsImRpc2NvdmVyeSciLCJ0ZWwgZGFuIiwidGVsIGRhbiBzdGVsZSIsImRhbiBzdGVsZSJd

[38] Collins, S., 2018, Tall el-Hamman Excavation Project, https://tallelhammam.com/

[39] Shanks, H., Commemorating a Covenant BAR 41:1 January/February 2015 https://www.baslibrary.org/biblical-archaeology-review/41/1/12

[40] BAR Staff 2012, Publishing Israel Archaeology Digs https://www.biblicalarchaeology.org/daily/archaeology-today/biblical-archaeology-topics/publishing-israel-archaeology-digs/

[41] BAR Staff 2012

[42] Wood, BG, 2008, Did the Israelites Conquer Jericho? A New Look at the Archaeological Evidence Associates for Biblical research https://biblearchaeology.org/research/conquest-of-canaan/2310-did-the-israelites-conquer-jericho-a-new-look-at-the-archaeological-evidence?highlight=WyJqZXJpY2hvIiwiamVyaWNobydzIiwiamVyaWNobyciLCInamVyaWNobyIsIidqZXJpY2hvJyJd

[43] BAR Staff 2012

[44] Shanks, H., 2010, Freeing the Dead Sea Scrolls, Continuum

[45] Smith, M.,, 2008, Why archaeologists need to publish outside of archaeology, Publishing Archaeology https://publishingarchaeology.blogspot.com/2008/11/why-archaeologists-need-to-publish.html

[46] NASA, 2003, A 'Smoking Gun' for Dinosaur Extinction https://www.jpl.nasa.gov/news/news.php?feature=8

[47] Ibid

[48] All About the Truth 2019, Israel History, https://www.allaboutthejourney.org/israel-history.htm

[49] All About the Truth 2019

[50] Philip, JC., & Cherian S., 2009 Analyzing Errors Of Interpretation

[51] Syro-Palestinian archaeology World Heritage Encyclopedia http://self.gutenberg.org/articles/Syro-Palestinian_archaeology

[52] Echard, A.,Biblical Archaeology FAQ CBN https://www1.cbn.com/biblestudy/biblical-archaeology-faq

[53] World Heritage Encyclopedia

[54] Ibid

[55] Landing Page, Associates for Biblical research 2019 https://biblearchaeology.org/

[56] Bible History Online 2019 https://www.bible-history.com/archaeology/

[57] Smith, H., 2006, Biblical Archaeology: Eternal Implications Associates for Biblical Research https://biblearchaeology.org/research/devotionals/4023-biblical-archaeology-eternal-implications?highlight=WyJiaWJsaWNhbCIsIidiaWJsaWNhbCIsIidiaWJsaWNhbCciLCJhcmNoYWVvbG9neSIsIidhcmNoYWVvbG9neSciLCJhcmNoYWVvbG9neSdzIiwiYXJjaGFlb2xvZ3kiIiwiJ2FyY2hhZW9sb2d5IiwiYXJjaGFlb2xvZ3knLiIsImV0ZXJuYWwiLCJpbXBsaWNhdGlvbnMiLCJiaWJsaWNhbCBhcmNoYWVvbG9neSIsImJpYmxpY2FsIG-FyY2hhZW9sb2d5IGV0ZXJuYWwiLCJhcmNoYWVvbG9neS-BldGVybmFsIiwiYXJjaGFlb2xvZ3kgZXRlcm5hbCBpbXBsaWNhdGlvbnMiLCJldGVybmFsIGltcGxpY2F0aW9ucyJd

[58] Johnstone, G, 2016, Pseudo-Archaeology http://www.archaeologyexpert.co.uk/PseudoArchaeology.html

[59] Fitzpatrick-Matthews, K., 2019, Bad Archaeology: what is it http://www.badarchaeology.com/what-is-it/

[60] Gates, 2017, Dangers of Pseudoarchaeology http://anthropology.msu.edu/anp364-fs17/2017/09/08/dangers-of-pseudoarchaeology/

[61] Fitzpatrick-Matthews, K., 2019

[62] Fitzpatrick-Matthews, K., 2019, http://www.badarchaeology.com/extraterrestrials/zecharia-sitchin/

[63] Fitzpatrick-Matthews, K., 2019, http://www.badarchaeology.com/religious-delusions/

[64] Gates 2017

[65] Woodward, C., 2009, The Mystery of Bosnia's Ancient Pyramids Smithsonian Magazine https://www.smithsonianmag.com/history/the-mystery-of-bosnias-ancient-pyramids-148990462/

[66] Harrison, RK, 2001, Old Testament Times Hendricksons Pub

[67] DHWTY 2019, Sargon of Akkad: Familiar and Legendary Tales of a Famous Mesopotamian King, Ancient Origins https://www.ancient-origins.net/history-famous-people/sargon-akkad-0010542

[68] Pearse, R., 2019, Mithras and Jesus http://www.tertullian.org/rpearse/mithras/display.php?page=Mithras_and_Jesus

[69] Tee, D., 2019, Moral Codes https://theologyarchaeology.wordpress.com/2014/04/24/moral-codes/

[70] Breed, B., 2019, How Was the Bible Written and Transmitted Bible Odyssey https://www.bibleodyssey.org/en/tools/bible-basics/how-was-the-bible-written-and-transmitted

[71] Chavalas, MW., & Younger Jr., Lawson, 2002, Mesopotamia and the Bible, Baker Academic

[72] IBid

[73] Thoma, PA., 2015, Mithraism, Ancient History Encyclopedia, https://www.ancient.eu/Mithraic_Mysteries/

[74] The Three Age System Bib-Arch, 2009 http://www.bibarch.com/Concepts/ArchPeriods.html

[75] Fitzpatrick-Matthews, K., 2007, The Three Age System, http://www.badarchaeology.com/the-history-of-archaeology/the-three-age-system/

[76] IBid

[77] The Art and Popular Culture Encyclopedia 2012, The Three Age System, http://www.artandpopularculture.com/Three-age_system

[78] Fitzpatrick-Matthews, K., 2007

[79] Bell, T., 2019, How to Calculate the Rate of Metal Corrosion https://www.thebalance.com/corrosion-rate-calculator-2339697

[80] IAA, 2019, The Israel Antiquities Authority - Vision and Goals http://www.antiquities.org.il/article_eng.aspx?sec_id=40&subj_id=226

[81] The SCA, 2019, Principal Mission http://www.sca-egypt.org/eng/main.html

[82] PP, 2019, What happens to finds, and who owns them http://www.pastperfect.org.uk/archaeology/metalfinds.html

[83] Fagan, B., 2008, Who Owns the Past, Brian Fagan Podcast The Rock Ethics Institute, https://rockethics.psu.edu/events/who-owns-the-past-an-archaeologist-looks-at-stakeholders-tourism-and-cultural-heritagethis-lecture-is-part-of-the-who-owns-our-species-past-present-future-lecture-series-1

[84] IBid

[85] Lacy, R., 2019, Ownership of the Grave: Who owns the Dead? https://spadeandthegrave.com/2019/11/08/ownership-of-the-grave-who-owns-the-dead/

[86] BAS Staff, 2012, Avraham Faust on David's Palace https://www.biblicalarchaeology.org/daily/archaeology-today/archaeologists-biblical-scholars-works/avraham-faust-on-davids-palace/

[87] Pettit, H., 2019, Lost Ancient Greek civilisation invented 'single-use cups The Sun https://www.thesun.co.uk/tech/10560485/ancient-greek-single-use-cups/

[88] Mandal, D., 2015, 4 remarkable inventions of Archimedes that still baffle us https://www.hexapolis.com/2015/07/07/4-remarkable-inventions-of-archimedes-that-still-baffle-us/2/

[89] Mandal, D., 2015

[90] Pellegrino, C., 1994, Return to Sodom & Gomorrah Random House. Also History of Math https://www.digitmath.com/babylonian-pythagorean-theorem-egyptian-mathematics.html

[91] IBid Pellegrino

[92] Pruitt, S., 2015, 8 Inventions We Owe to the Ancients History https://www.history.com/news/8-inventions-we-owe-to-the-ancients

[93] IBid

[94] Pruitt, S., 2015

[95] Pellegrino, C.,

[96] Mykytiuk, L., 2017,53 People in the Bible Confirmed Archaeologically BAR, https://www.biblicalarchaeology.org/daily/people-cultures-in-the-bible/people-in-the-bible/50-people-in-the-bible-confirmed-archaeologically/?mqsc=E3862893&utm_source=WhatCountsE-mail&utm_medium=BHDWeek%20in%20Review%20Newsletter&utm_campaign=E6WD17

[97] Tee, D., 2017, Biblical Archaeology Discoveries Theologyarchaeology https://theologyarchaeology.wordpress.com/2017/06/27/biblical-archaeology-discoveries/

[98] Bruce, FF., 1958, Archaeological Confirmation of the New Testament Carl F.H. Henry, ed.,

Revelation and the Bible. Contemporary Evangelical Thought. Grand Rapids: Baker,

[99] American Heritage® Dictionary of the English Language, Fifth Edition. Copyright © 2016 by Houghton Mifflin Harcourt Publishing Company. Published by Houghton Mifflin Harcourt Publishing Company. All rights reserved. https://www.thefreedictionary.com/confirmation

[100] Collins English Dictionary - Complete & Unabridged 2012 Digital Edition

© William Collins Sons & Co. Ltd. 1979, 1986 © HarperCollins Publishers 1998, 2000, 2003, 2005, 2006, 2007, 2009, 2012 https://www.dictionary.com/browse/affirm

[101] Leeder III, H., 2017, Does archeology prove the Bible is true https://yellowhammernews.com/does-archeology-prove-the-bible-is-true/

[102] Eames, C., 2019, The Vital Importance of Biblical Archaeology, Watch Jerusalem https://watchjerusalem.co.il/747-the-vital-importance-of-biblical-archaeology

[103] IBid

[104] Eames , C., 2019 Watch Jerusalem

[105] Morrow, JL., 2016, On Biblical Scholarship and Bias, Bible Interp http://bibleinterp.com/articles/2016/12/mor408020.shtml

[106] Finkelstein , I., & Silbermann, NA., 2007, David & Solomon, Free Press

[107] Ibid

[108] Seiglie, M., 2009, The Exodus Controversy, Associates for Biblical Research   https://biblearchaeology.org/research/founder-s-corner/ 2288-the-exodus-controversy

[109] Davies, PR., 1992, What do we mean by "ISRAEL" http://vri-dar.info/bibarch/arch/davies4.htm

[110] Davies, PR., 1992

[111] Sala, HJ., 2018, Can You trust the Bible OMF Literature Ch. 3

[112] Wood, B., 2008, The Walls of Jericho Associates for Biblical Research   https://biblearchaeology.org/research/conquest-of-canaan/ 3625-the-walls-of-jericho?highlight=WyJqZXJpY2hvIiwiamVyaWNoby-dzIiwiamVyaWNobyciLCInamVyaWNobyIsIidqZXJpY2hvJyJd

[113] Wood, B., 2008

[114] TLloyd, E., 2019, The Hittites – Rise And Fall Of An Ancient Powerful Empire In Anatolia, Ancient Pages http://www.ancient-pages.com/2019/02/18/the-hittites-rise-and-fall-of-an-ancient-powerful-empire-in-anatolia/

[115] Lloyd, E., 2019 Ancient Pages

[116] Zonszein, M., 2014, Domesticated Camels Came to Israel in 930 B.C., Centuries Later Than Bible Says National Geographic https://www.nationalgeographic.com/news/2014/2/140210-domesticat-ed-camels-israel-bible-archaeology-science/

[117] Zonszein, M., 2014 National Geographic

[118] Sala, HJ., 2018 OMF Literature Ch. 3

[119] Schlenoff, D., 2014, Lawrence in Arabia: from Archaeologist to Spy, 1914, Scientific American https://blogs.scientificamerican.com/anec-

dotes-from-the-archive/lawrence-in-arabia-from-archaeologist-to-spy-1914/

[120] Way., K., 2014, Is the Bible Wrong about Camels in Genesis? The Good Book Blog

Talbot School of Theology https://www.biola.edu/blogs/good-book-blog/2014/is-the-bible-wrong-about-camels-in-genesis